The
POWER
of
GOD'S LOVE

Other Books by Dr. Charles F. Stanley

The POWER *of* GOD'S LOVE

A 31-Day Devotional to Discover
the Father's Greatest Gift

DR. CHARLES F. STANLEY

NELSON
BOOKS

An Imprint of Thomas Nelson

Published in Nashville, Tennessee, by Nelson Books, an imprint of Thomas Nelson. Nelson Books and Thomas Nelson are registered trademarks of HarperCollins Christian Publishing, Inc.

Thomas Nelson titles may be purchased in bulk for educational, business, fund-raising, or sales promotional use. For information, please e-mail SpecialMarkets@ ThomasNelson.com.

Unless otherwise noted, Scripture quotations are taken from the NEW AMERICAN STANDARD BIBLE®, © The Lockman Foundation 1960, 1962, 1963, 1968, 1971, 1972, 1973, 1975, 1977, 1995. Used by permission.

Scripture quotations marked NIV are from the HOLY BIBLE: NEW INTERNATIONAL VERSION®. © 1973, 1978, 1984 by International Bible Society. Used by permission of Zondervan Publishing House. All rights reserved.

ISBN 978-0-7180-8662-6 (custom)

Library of Congress Cataloging-in-Publication Data

Stanley, Charles F.
    The power of God's love : a 31-day devotional to discover the Father's
greatest gift / Charles F. Stanley.
        p. cm.
    ISBN 978-1-4002-0093-1
    1. God (Christianity)—Love—Meditations. I. Title.
BT140.S7198 2008
231'.6—dc22

                                                    2008003398

Printed in the United States of America

18 19 20 RRD 7 6 5 4 3

God is love, and the one
who abides in love abides in God,
and God abides in him.
1 John 4:16

CONTENTS

LOVE SO AMAZING

What is the deepest need in your life? Some may say more money, another job, a new car, a larger home, a greater feeling of security, or any number of things. However, if we are truly honest, most of us would agree that the greatest need we have is to be loved unconditionally. This is a basic need that each one of us has. In fact, God created us in love—to be loved and to love others.

Years ago, a country singer wrote a song that proclaimed he had been looking for love in all the wrong places. Today, these few words have become somewhat of a chilling cliché because far too many people are doing just that—looking for love in all the wrong places. People are searching for love that will last and not fade, but they are not looking to God—the only One who knows how to love them unconditionally.

Many mistakenly believe that if they gain a new position in life, they will have fulfillment and then feel loved. Some think money is the answer to every need they have. They conclude that having more of it will yield less emptiness. However, emptiness of heart and soul can never be satisfied with a few extra dollars—or for that matter, even millions. Having more of anything does not mean we will gain the type of love that we were created to enjoy.

There also are people who have never learned how to love. They do not know how to love themselves, God, or others. They may have grown up feeling unloved by their parents—not knowing if they would be embraced or pushed away. They realize something is broken inside their hearts, but they do not know how to fix it. So they give up on love. Others have genuinely tried to love, but they have been deeply hurt and painfully rejected over and over again. They pull down the emotional shades of their lives and isolate their hearts so they will not be hurt again.

Countless people enter marriage relationships carrying with them much more than suitcases of clothes. They have emotional baggage left over from previous relationships that did not work out. The scars of hurt within their lives are deep, and now they are looking to their new spouse to meet their needs and remove their emotional pain. This will never happen because there is only one Person who can meet every need we have— and that is Jesus Christ. The intimacy we can enjoy with Him through a personal relationship is far greater than anything this world has to offer. And learning the right way to love God prepares us to express love and then to receive it.

In the eighteenth century, Isaac Watts wrote the words to a song that we often sing at Easter. I want to share just a portion of it with you as a testimony of love and pure devotion to the Savior—the Person who has promised to love you no matter where you have been or what you have done. In the hymn "When I Survey the Wondrous Cross," Watts wrote these touching words: "Were the whole realm of nature mine, that were a present far too small; love so amazing, so divine, demands my soul, my life, my all."

Have you ever known love so great that it leaves you speechless, motionless, and longing to have more of it? This is the love that God has for you to experience. Only when you come to know His love will your longing be satisfied.

You may have picked up this book thinking, *If only I could know what it felt like to be loved by God*. I want to assure you, there is a way. Or perhaps you saw the title of this book and thought, *I've tried to love, and I have only faced one hurt after another. I don't want to go through that again*. God knows the hurts you have faced, and He promises to heal the wounds of your soul.

You may be someone who already knows the embrace of perfect love, and you want to grow deeper in your affection for God. If this is the case, He has a pool of refreshment waiting for you, and He will walk alongside it with you.

True love is waiting for you. I want to challenge you to read the words of this book with a new perspective—

one that is not based on past experience or a preconceived thought about the love of God. Instead, my prayer is that you will find a quiet place to retreat to for a few minutes each day for the next thirty-one days and allow the One who loves you perfectly to speak to your heart and whisper words of His unending devotion to you.

—Charles F. Stanley

EVERLASTING LOVE

I have loved you with an everlasting love;
therefore I have drawn you with lovingkindness.
—Jer. 31:3

What if you could know that no matter what you have done, you are loved unconditionally? Many people find this hard to imagine; they live each day with a heavy sense of guilt over past sins and failures. They feel as though they will never be able to meet the expectations of others, including their spouses, employers, family members, friends, and especially God.

Far too often, we hear about the love of God and think secretly, *Oh, but you don't know what I have done. God could never love me, much less accept me.* The awesome truth is this: He loves you unconditionally and also eternally. He loves you the way you are. He created you in love and He has promised to love you forever.

Does He love sin, brokenness of heart, and actions that prevent you from knowing Him personally? No, because He knows that each one of these has the potential to wreck and ruin your life while preventing you from experiencing His love in a personal way. No matter what experiences or feelings you have had, God loves you and this will never change.

You may have grown up in a home where you felt unloved, overlooked, and dismissed. This is not true with God. When He sees your life—no matter how young or old you are—He sees potential, promise, hope, and someone He has created in His own image. He loves you.

When you make wrong choices and drift in your devotion to Him, His love will not grow cold. It remains red hot with devotion. Though there are consequences to sin, God will never stop pursuing you, seeking to bring you back to Him.

Maybe you have chosen to walk away from Him, feeling as though you cannot live up to His standards. No one can; we all need His help, His guidance, His compassion, and most of all, His unending love.

Perhaps you have faced one rejection after another, and it seems as though there is little in life that you want to live for. Remember this: God knows the struggles of your heart. He hears your cries, and if you will turn to Him, He will answer your prayers, heal your brokenness, bring a sense of overwhelming joy to your life, and never leave you.

He won't withhold His love from you. In fact, nothing can stop or prevent the love of God. There is no sin too great for His love to overcome. Love is what changes us and draws us closer to Him than we ever believed possible—His divine love that forgives, restores, renews, and reenergizes. Sin may blind you to God's personal care and compassion, but it is powerless in His presence.

After His death, Jesus' disciples became frightened and wondered if they would soon lose their lives as well. They scattered in fear, and most returned to their former way of life. Peter, James, and John were no exceptions. After His resurrection, Jesus came to them and found them out on the open Sea of Galilee, tossing their nets into the water, hoping to catch a day's wages of fish (John 21).

They had lost their eternal perspective of the power of His love. They had forgotten His words and turned to their own resources. Yet, at the sight of the risen Savior, their hope was renewed, their passion rekindled, and their dreams reborn. Do you feel as though your hopes have been dashed, your dreams have been shattered, and the fire of your passion has been blown out?

The moment these men saw Jesus standing on the shore, Peter jumped into the water and began swimming to Him, and the others followed in the boat. They realized their fears were imagined. God had done exactly what He promised to do, and the same is true concerning your life. The Lord will never abandon you, will never stop loving you, and will always seek to draw closer to you.

Jesus came to earth to save us from an eternal death. He also came to break the power of sin. This means you can say no to the very things that have separated you from God and yes to an eternity of joy, peace, promise, and love!

God, help me to understand the depth of Your love. I know in my mind that You love me, but I want to experience Your love with my heart and soul, not simply read about it or examine it in a Bible study. Draw me into Your love and keep me there.

Amen.

AN ETERNAL NEED

The one who does not love does not know God, for God is love.
—*1 John 4:8*

What is the strongest motivation in your life? If you could list one thing that is at the center of your focus, what would it be? Some people are motivated by their jobs, the pursuit of material gain, or a relationship. Jesus, however, had an entirely different perspective on this subject. In Matthew 6, He tells us, "Do not worry then, saying, 'What will we eat?' or 'What will we drink?' or 'What will we wear for clothing?' For the Gentiles eagerly seek all these things; for your heavenly Father knows that you need all these things. But seek first His kingdom and His righteousness, and all these things will be added to you" (vv. 31–33). In other words, set the focus of your heart on Christ, and everything you truly need will be given to you.

The list Jesus gives in this passage is not limited to these items alone. The fact is, anything that blocks our view of God has the potential to prevent us from following Him in faith. He knows the needs we have and has promised to meet each one (see Phil. 4:19). However, many people begin to see their personal desires as needs that must be met immediately. They are on a quest to achieve and gain more of everything. They fail to realize the danger that is lurking—one that will consume their hearts and minds—if they are not careful.

A desire for a greater position, more fame, or more money can lead to a lack of trust in God. It can also open the door to discontentment, frustration, and anger. Often, our desires boil down to one thing: the more we have as a result of our own striving, the less we need God. While there is nothing wrong with enjoying the blessings God gives us—material or otherwise—there is a warning that we need to heed whenever we begin to value His blessings more than we do our relationship with Him.

You know you are headed for trouble when you sense your life is spinning out of control. You are running and rushing in all directions with no time set aside to be alone with the Lord. Each one of us was created with a need to be with Him. We can never learn how to love others, ourselves, and most of all Him unless we first experience the joy of being in His presence.

Some people are driven by a sense of fear, greed, or lust. They also are blinded to the goodness and mercy of a loving God, who only wants one thing: a personal relationship with them. When we open our hearts to Christ, we learn to live differently each day. Instead of counting on what we can do as a result of our effort, we pray and ask God to do for us what only He can. There is a huge difference between living for yourself in your own ability and living with God's infinite resources.

First Corinthians 13 is sometimes referred to as the "love chapter" of the Bible. In it, the apostle Paul talks about the supremacy of love over knowledge, and about faith, generosity, and even the ultimate sacrifice of one's life. He explains genuine love—that it is patient, kind, humble, polite, not jealous, not self-seeking, not easily provoked, keeps no record of wrongs, rejoices in truth, bears all things, believes all things, hopes all things, and never fails.

In fact, the Bible tells us God *is* love (1 John 4:8). When you trusted Jesus Christ as your personal Savior, the Holy Spirit came to live within you. Literally, you have been given God's ability to love the way He loves. As you surrender yourself to Him, His divine love flows through you. You are no longer left alone to make crucial decisions about the future—what to do or where to live and work. Whatever needs arise, God provides the wisdom you need to make the right decision every time.

Jesus told His followers, "As the Father has loved Me, I have also loved you; abide in My love" (John 15:9). The love of God the Father for His Son and the love of the Son for His Father are available to every Christian. God invites you through faith in His Son to live in this very love—His love—every day.

Lord, thank You for the devotion of Your Son Jesus Christ. Thank You for the example He is to me of Your unfailing love. Thank You that I can know Your love in the way that He did. Help me to love You in return, in a Christlike way.

Amen.

LOVE THAT HEALS

*"The LORD is near to the brokenhearted
and saves those who are crushed in spirit."*
—Ps. 34:18

Have you ever tottered on the edge of despair, so
disillusioned and disheartened that you wondered if God
really loved you? Have you been so wounded by painful
circumstances or a loved one's careless actions that you
questioned if God could really heal your hurt?

All of us have experienced the anguish that comes
from such moments. And if our perspective on the love
of Christ is clouded, we may give in to feelings of doubt,
depression, bitterness, and fear. How grateful I am that
our Savior comes to our aid, offering His tender love and
understanding in times of brokenness and deep sorrow.

In describing the hurt that the Savior experienced
during His earthly ministry, the prophet Isaiah wrote,

"He will not cry out or raise His voice, nor make His voice heard in the street. A bruised reed he will not break, a dimly burning wick he will not extinguish." (Isaiah 42:2–3) Jesus changed their dreary, desperate world into one of renewed hope and confidence. And the healing power of His love can change your world too.

If you feel like a "bruised reed" about to break or a "dimly burning wick," take courage. The love of God is both strong and tender enough to heal your hurts and revive your spirit. At your weakest moment, God's love is completely sufficient to sustain you. You can count on God's tender mercy to restore you in your darkest hours.

God's love is infinite, and nothing can stand in its way, however great our sin or small our faith.

Heavenly Father, life can be difficult, and at times I feel beaten down by adversity. I wonder where You are and if You hear my prayers—yet I know in my heart that You do. Please strengthen my faith today, and renew my faith in You.

UNFAILING LOVE

We have thought on Your lovingkindness,
O God, in the midst of Your temple.
—Ps. 48:9

For years, I have read the Psalms almost every day as a part of my time spent with God. It seems as though each time I read them, I discover a new principle, truth, or blessing. David wrote at length about God's unfailing love, and his words of truth offer real strength and comfort for the difficult times we are sure to face.

The writers of the Old Testament used the Hebrew word *checed* to express God's care for His children. This word is often translated into "lovingkindness" or "steadfast love," which conveys the permanence of God's unconditional love for us.

Unlike the love we show to one another, God's love

is infinite and powerful enough to forgive the most grievous wrong. It endures life's greatest hardships and heals the deepest wounds. The steadfast love of God never changes, is never diminished by our behavior, and is never lessened by our indifference or even rebellion. Christ's love has no boundaries—it persists through all of our circumstances and through all time. The writer of Hebrews translates God's devotion this way: "I will never desert you, nor will I ever forsake you" (13:5).

Since God's love for us is unfailing and unchanging, we can rest in complete assurance of His faithfulness. King David—whose life was constantly in peril—wrote, "The king trusts in the LORD, and through the lovingkindness of the Most High he will not be shaken" (Ps. 21:7). Can you say the same thing? David faced times of unbelievable stress. Though he had been anointed king of Israel, David was forced to leave his home and family and live on the run in fear of a madman who was determined to kill him. Yet his faith and trust rested securely in God's remarkable love for him—and so can yours. When you feel shaken by the circumstances of life, remember that you have an unshakable God covering you with His all-powerful wings of protection.

There is a secret strength that is yours to discover. The one thing that has stabilized my life through all these years is the quiet time I spend with God every day—every morning. The psalmist prayed to the Lord, "O satisfy us in the morning with Your lovingkindness, that we may sing for joy and be glad all our days" (Ps. 90:14).

If you start each morning meditating on God's unfailing love, your life will change forever. Instead of getting up and wondering how you will get through the day, you will get up with a sense of expectancy and hope because, when you seek God, you will find Him. In fact, the more time you spend with Him, the more you will come to know His boundless love, and the more joy you will experience. The more joyful you are, the more exciting your walk with Christ will become and the more dynamic your faith will be. God blesses those who seek Him. He came looking for Adam in the cool of the day, and He is waiting for you even now.

The steadfast love of Christ is our anchor for every

storm and what satisfies the deepest longing of our hearts.

Heavenly Father, I can hardly imagine what Your unfailing, unceasing love really means. I do know that it is what I yearn for in my heart. Each day, grant me a more complete understanding of how much You really love me. Along the way, teach me how to express that love to those around me. Thank You for creating the need for love within me and supplying that need.

Amen.

RECEIVING GOD'S LOVE

His lovingkindness is great toward us.
—Ps. 117:2

One of the first verses of Scripture I learned as a young Christian—and probably the verse most believers learn—is John 3:16: "For God so loved the world, that He gave His only begotten Son, that whoever believes in Him shall not perish, but have eternal life." This is one of the best places to start when we think of God's love because it teaches us that His love is sacrificial—given to us as an act of grace and without hesitation.

No one loves you more than Jesus—no friend, parent, or spouse. His love supersedes all we can know or understand. As I have grown in Christ, I have come to understand that the entire Bible is the revelation of God's love for us. From Genesis to Revelation, it is the story of God's persistent desire to redeem and reconcile human beings to an eternal fellowship with Him.

Why then do we develop such stubborn resistance to receiving and enjoying His love? Why do so many Christians live with feelings of self-condemnation, fear, and doubt? If God loves us unconditionally, is it possible to enjoy this love without fear of losing it? Yes! He never extends His love only to withdraw it when we do something wrong. He is not looking for ways to punish us. Satan, however, is constantly at work behind the scenes, whispering words of condemnation in order to discourage us. He will try anything to tempt us into believing that we can actually lose the love of God when nothing could be further from the truth.

Once God saves you, He gives you all that He has to give. You may spend a lifetime learning how to live and walk in the light of His love, but you will never be unloved by Him. Stronger than any earthly vow, His vow of love to you is forever. "I will not fail you or forsake you" (Josh. 1:5), and He never will.

We learn of His love through prayer, the study of

His Word, and the sermons we hear at church. However, many times the depth of His love fails to resonate in our hearts because we have become prideful and self-reliant, and we do not believe we need His help.

Thankfully, His powerful love can reach beyond every barrier of pride and bring us to a place of true humility. Jesus said, "Just as the Father has loved Me, I have also loved you; abide in My love" (John 15:9). He used the Greek word *agape*—a word seldom used by the Greeks—that expresses the concept of absolute adoration.

Unconditional love means this: God loves you just the way you are. Isn't that something we all long for, to be loved without conditions or stipulations? He loves you when you obey, and He loves you when you rebel. That doesn't mean He tolerates sin—He died because of it—or that He minimizes its consequences. But it does mean that His love for you is steadfast regardless of your actions.

However much you have come to depend upon yourself, it is never too late to put your faith in Christ.

21

When you do, His agape love will transform your life completely. He loves you as much now as He ever will, and His love comes with no strings attached—it is a free gift, given from a pure heart. This may sound too good to be true, but it isn't. Receive it, accept it, and you will never again be the same.

Heavenly Father, I have relied upon myself for so long that it is difficult to trust someone else with my life—yet I choose to do that today. I place my hope in You. Show me the places in my heart where pride has taken root, and help me to surrender them to You. As I humble myself, reveal Your words of love throughout Scripture so I may be solidly grounded in an understanding of Your agape love.

Amen.

THE CURE OF GRACE

We have peace with God through our Lord Jesus Christ, through whom also we have obtained our introduction by faith into this grace in which we stand.
—Rom. 5:1–2

I admit that I like setting goals for my life. I also enjoy what I do through the ministry and have often told my family, friends, and church congregation that I cannot imagine retiring. Though God may bring a shift into my life at some point, I want to continue working and serving Him until the day I die. When I hear people talking about retirement and just being able to do nothing, I always think, *That's just not for me.* I love life, people, and being involved with God's work.

While there is nothing inherently wrong with this mindset, sometimes it can lead to problems. This is why I always counsel others to be balanced with their goals, expectations, and, most of all, faithfulness in their devotion to the Lord. When God makes it clear that you need to step away to a quiet place to be alone with Him, you need to do it.

Staying in tune with His Spirit is the key to avoiding feelings of being overwhelmed or burned out. Years ago, I learned this the hard way. I had been through a particularly difficult season of stress. I was striving to please those around me and, admittedly, to please God. I had forgotten that there was nothing I could do to become more acceptable to the Lord. He already had proclaimed His unconditional acceptance of me (Rom. 15:7).

I also knew He was asking me to draw aside from my busy routine to be alone with Him. Yet I kept pushing in my effort to reach certain goals and to do certain duties. As the pastor of an ever-changing and growing church, I felt as though I needed to be all things to all people.

My family could see the crash coming, but I refused to take time to be still and quiet and to just allow God to renew and refresh me. Finally, He got my full attention, and I agreed to take time off. God used this time to refocus my life on Him and to set a spiritual course for me to follow the rest of my days.

I personally learned that His grace was sufficient for every need I had (2 Cor. 12:9). During this time, His Word became even sweeter to me. And I learned a powerful lesson: in His presence, there is an abundant sense of acceptance, rest, and unconditional love for all of us who keep going past the point where God says, "Stop and be with Me for a while." King David understood the wisdom that came from being with the Lord. In Psalm 23, he wrote, "The LORD is my shepherd . . . He makes me lie down in green pastures; He leads me beside quiet waters. He restores my soul" (vv. 1–3).

God's grace is an important reality to understand and receive. John tells us that Jesus was "full of grace and truth" (John 1:14). His message to the apostles was the triumph of grace over law. Apart from the cornerstone of grace, the gospel would be fundamentally flawed. We cannot understand Christianity or the love of Christ until we experience His grace up close and personal.

What is grace? It is God's love and kindness toward

humanity without regard for the worth or merit of those who receive it—and in spite of the fact that we don't deserve it. Because of His grace, we cannot do anything to make Him love us any less or any more than He does.

When we fully grasp this reality, our tiresome efforts to perform in order to earn His love fade. We don't have to be successful to be loved by God. We are redeemed by the sacrifice of Jesus Christ, and that is a free gift for everyone willing to accept it—we can do nothing to merit it.

Unfortunately, many people are so used to earning the acceptance of their peers that they try to do the same with God. But His grace goes completely against this notion. We don't have to do anything to deserve God's affection; we are pleasing to Him because Christ died for our sins.

Are you working hard to gain God's favor or the favor of others? Is there always something more you think you have to do to be accepted? God has done all you need through the cross of Christ to make you acceptable.

Ephesians 2:8–9 tells us, "By grace you have been

saved through faith; and that not of yourselves, it is the gift of God; not as a result of works, so that no one may boast." When Paul wrote to Timothy, he encouraged the young man to find his strength in God's grace alone (2 Tim. 2:1). Christ's work on the cross has been credited to your account so you can live abundantly—free from sin and guilt (John 10:10).

Lord, please help me to understand the principle of Your grace at work in my life. For so long, I have tried to be a good person, but nothing has ever worked. I kept making the same mistakes. Now I realize it is only by Your grace and unconditional love that I am saved from sin. Please show me how to draw even closer to You so that I can experience the fullness of Your love and blessing.

Amen.

PERFECT LOVE

This is love, not that we loved God, but that He loved us
and sent His Son to be the propitiation for our sins.
—*1 John 4:10*

Love is the greatest gift God offers us, and yet it is the one we have the most difficulty receiving. Why? First of all, we do not think we deserve His love, which is fundamentally true. However, because God created us in love, He loves us without hesitation. Because He is love, it is His nature to love. In fact, there is nothing strong enough to stop Him from loving us.

Second, more than likely, most of us face times when we find it hard to accept or understand the love of God because there simply is nothing on earth that compares to it. We continue to believe He loves us the way we love others, which is wrong. Often our love is conditional, but God's love is unconditional. When we compare the love of God to our own human love, we are tempted to doubt His promise to us—to love us regardless of what we do or don't do.

God's love is not based on emotion, as human love often is. It is based on His character, His nature, and His supreme desire to love each one of us with an everlasting love. The Bible tells us, "God is love" (1 John 4:8). Since it is impossible for Him to do anything contrary to His nature, His love is certain, sure, and eternal.

In addition, His love is a gift. James tells us, "Every good thing given and every perfect gift is from above, coming down from the Father of lights, with whom there is no variation or shifting shadow" (1:17). In other words, God's love is unchanging and independent of our feelings about deserving it. We cannot earn it or give anything in return for it—God's gift is something He offers freely.

Furthermore, the love of our heavenly Father is perfect. God is the absolute perfection of every aspect of His character. For example, His power is perfect power, just as His knowledge is perfect knowledge. Every one of His attributes is the peak of perfection and cannot be improved upon to any degree. Since His love is perfect, we know it will certainly benefit us. He always will treat us in accordance with His love.

I can remember a time when I was really struggling with a circumstance in my life. I had become impatient, as we all do on occasion. One particular morning, I was so overwhelmed that I knelt by the bed and poured out my heart to God, asking Him, "Why don't You just get on with this?" And then it was as if God whispered to me, "You can trust perfect love." All of a sudden, my burden left, my frustration disappeared, and my anxiety vanished.

My understanding of God's love took a big step forward that day. It was suddenly clear that His love is trustworthy in any and every situation of life. Whatever you are facing, no matter how you are feeling, God is loving you . . . perfectly.

Dear heavenly Father, Your love for me is perfect, and yet I so often forget that. Please help me to trust You completely—regardless of the situations I find myself in. Help me to understand Your love fully and to put my trust in You.

Amen.

LOVING YOUR ENEMIES

Love your enemies, and do good.
—Luke 6:35

One of the most challenging times of my life came as a result of my obedience to God. Early in my ministry at First Baptist Church of Atlanta, I faced a serious time of conflict. What first appeared to be a low point in ministry actually became an opportunity for personal growth, change, and renewal. It also provided an opportunity for members of my congregation to develop a deeper devotion to God.

As the situation grew more difficult with each day, I quickly realized I could respond either through my flesh—becoming angry or frustrated—or by allowing God's love to work through me, and, in doing so, demonstrate His amazing ability to bring unity instead of conflict. I chose to respond in love through faith in God. At times, His command to love our enemies may seem impossible. But through the love of Christ, we can override our emotions and prime our wills to obey Him. Every time we do, He brings a wondrous blessing into our lives.

As I read about David's awkward relationship with King Saul, I realized that God was showing me how to treat those who hurt or mistreat us. Thoroughly misunderstood and relentlessly pursued, David spent years running in fear of his enemies—hiding in caves and wildernesses in an effort to escape Saul and his army, who were committed to killing him. Twice he had an opportunity to slay his tormentor. Yet he refused to exercise the option of hate, choosing instead to demonstrate his innocence and loyalty.

He did not retaliate, and if we are wise, we will travel the same route. Anytime we seek revenge—subtly or blatantly—we hinder the power of God's love. Retaliation takes the matter out of God's providential hand and puts it in our sinful grasp. It violates His law of love, which Peter defines this way: "[Do] not [return] evil for evil or insult for insult, but giving a blessing instead" (1 Pet. 3:9).

How do you avoid answering the blow you have received? You do this by taking refuge in the shadow of God's all-powerful wings. David writes, "It is He who delivers you from the snare of the trapper and from the deadly pestilence. He will cover you with His pinions, and under His wings you may seek refuge; His faithfulness is a shield and bulwark" (Ps. 91:3–4).

You also learn how to endure persecution by recalling the words Peter wrote concerning Christ's death on the cross: "He did not revile [retaliate] in return; while suffering, He uttered no threats, but kept entrusting Himself to Him who judges righteously" (1 Pet. 2:23). Both David and the Lord Jesus made God their hiding place from the schemes of wicked men, trusting Him to handle their hurts.

Entrusting yourself and your particular circumstance to God frees you to extend grace to the offending party. Love flowed from the cross. David spoke graciously and courteously to Saul. We should do the same to those who wrong us. When this seems difficult to do, it is because you are trying to do this in your own ability. Instead, ask God to speak through you—to love, forgive, and even honor your accuser or offender through you. When you speak kindly to those who hurt you, the overwhelming thought of retaliation will fade, and the love of God will take its place.

The noblest expression of love is to give it to those who do not deserve it. That is what Jesus did when He gave Himself up for us, and we are called to be like Him. Love your enemies, and your faith will grow stronger. You can do it because God loved you first.

Lord, I admit that it is sometimes hard to love others when they wrong me. My natural response is to distance myself from them or somehow retaliate. I ask You to prompt my spirit to react with kindness when someone offends me. I know that I can do this only through the strength of Your Holy Spirit.

Amen.

THE BIG PICTURE

Man looks at the outward appearance,
but the LORD looks at the heart.
—1 Sam. 16:7

We gain great insight from the people we read about in the Bible. Many times, we see them as being different from ourselves—having had more talent, patience, ability, and love for God. However, most of them were ordinary and not so different from us. Moses and Peter had very humble beginnings. Just like us, David encountered many serious obstacles—some were of his own doing. The common lives of these people tell us a great deal about the Christian faith and our own ability to live it. Through reading Scripture, we can see clearly that God is equally as interested in the process of our lives as He is in the final result.

Those who trust in Christ as their Savior will arrive

safely in heaven. However, there is even more to be gained by living each day in faith and trust in Christ. Jesus' sacrifice on the cross settles the issue of our salvation. However, during our short time on earth, the process of making us more like His Son is God's primary objective.

Our spiritual development involves times of failure and success, joy and grief, wisdom and foolishness, peace and turmoil. In fact, if you were to chart the spiritual courses that Moses and David took, you would see many highs and lows. Becoming like Jesus is a lifelong endeavor that involves advancement as well as setbacks.

If you are facing a time of confusion or failure in your walk with the Lord, do not become discouraged. God trains us for service by disciplining us when we take a wrong turn. Like a gentle but firm and loving Father, He loves us but corrects our sinful behavior. What may seem painful now will become an opportunity for celebration later.

One young man whom I counseled told how he almost became discouraged. He admitted that he had wrongly handled the financial funds that God had given him. Then he proceeded to ignore the bills that arrived at the end of each month. Just as creditors were about to turn him over to debt collectors, he realized that what he was doing was wrong and turned to financial counseling.

However, this one step did not prevent his debtors from calling. They wanted their money, and they wanted it now. "Haven't I been obedient to God?" he asked me. For the moment he had, but he also had forgotten that sin has consequences.

As we grow in our walk with the Lord, we begin to turn to Him for wisdom and advice: "Lord, show me Your way in these circumstances before I make a mistake and have to suffer the consequences of a wrong decision." When you pray this prayer, God will guide you, but you also must be willing to wait for His answer. Sometimes it comes immediately, and other times it comes when He knows it is best for you to hear what He has to say.

God always is more concerned with our progress than He is our comfort. The men and women whom

He used historically and the people He uses today are far from faultless. What God does care about is a heart that is bent toward obedience to Him—repentant when wrong, contrite when disobedient, and humble when self-reliant. Although our spiritual progress will include times of failure, this moves us closer in our relationship with the Savior.

The Lord's love for David did not change even when he failed because David's heart was set on Him. God saw David's potential for godliness and waited patiently for it to develop. What farmer discards a half-grown crop? He waters, watches, and protects it until harvest. When God saves you, He knows your tremendous spiritual potential. Peter's initial hesitation paled in comparison to his later loyalty and commitment. Moses' forty years of exile were merely preparation for forty years of tough leadership.

If you know God is interested in the process, looks for ultimate progress, and sees unlimited potential, you can be liberated to walk and act under the umbrella of His love. God's commitment to you is for eternity, and

He is with you today to help you make the most of each opportunity. If you falter or fail, He will correct you and help you walk upright again.

Gracious Father, I am so grateful that You see my life from an eternal perspective and that You have a magnificent plan for me. And as much as I do not like valley experiences, I know they teach me more about Your faithfulness than I could ever learn by living a life free of trial and struggle. Thank You for not giving up on me, for being so good to me, and for having a big picture in mind for my life.

Amen.

LOVE'S PARDON

Though your sins are as scarlet, they will be as white as snow;
though they are red like crimson, they will be like wool.
—Isa. 1:18

One day while working in my darkroom printing several photographs I had taken, I made an interesting discovery. Occasionally when photographing in black and white, I use colored filters over my camera lenses. A light yellow filter darkens the sky while brightening the clouds. A red filter enhances anything that is white. On this particular day, I experimented with viewing a red dot on white paper through a red filter. To my amazement, the dot, when seen through the red filter, appeared white.

Immediately, I thought of Isaiah's words: "Though your sins are as scarlet, they will be as white as snow; though they are red like crimson, they will be like wool" (Isa. 1:18). Our sin, depicted as deep red by Isaiah, becomes white as snow and wool when seen through the red cross of Golgotha. This is the great transformation of forgiveness. Jesus, the Lamb of God, took away our iniquity when His blood was shed on the cross. Our past sins, today's transgressions, and tomorrow's disobedience have been fully forgiven by Christ's once-and-for-all sacrifice.

By His own doing, God in Christ has cleansed you from every stain of transgression. Though you may still suffer some of the damaging consequences of past sin, the heavenly Father never treats you as anything other than His beloved child who has a bright and glorious future. You are a new creation in Christ—a saint created in the image of His Son.

God's forgiveness not only takes your sins away but also credits the righteousness of Christ to your account. Years ago, Corrie ten Boom, who was an author, speaker, and former prisoner of a Nazi prison camp, wrote in *A Tramp for the Lord* a very simple but perfect explanation of God's ability to forgive and forget: "Our sins are now cast into the deepest sea and a sign is put up that says, 'No Fishing Allowed'."

We often overlook this principle when thinking about the subject of forgiveness. Satan loves to accuse us and remind us of past deeds that God has dealt with and forgiven, but the apostle Paul tells us, "There is now no condemnation for those who are in Christ Jesus" (Rom. 8:1). No blame can ever be charged to your account because you have been justified, declared "not guilty" by the Judge of the universe—God Himself.

He freely expresses the fullness of His love to you because there is no barrier—justice has been satisfied. His complete forgiveness, freely given, erases all guilt. The Holy Spirit will indeed convict you of sin, but if you receive His forgiveness, you will never stand guilty before God.

This is how God sees you: pure as snow, white as wool. Your sins have been permanently cleansed through the shed blood of Christ. Since this is how He views you, shouldn't you see yourself in the same light?

Father, I can witness Your miracles and promises being fulfilled by simply opening my eyes to Your creation every day. Knowing that You see me as pure, whole, and blameless is a miracle in itself. I want to thank You and praise You for Your perfect, living example of love.

Amen.

LEARNING TO LET GO

My times are in Your hand.
—Ps. 31:15

Do you sometimes wrestle with God over an issue you desperately want solved? Most of us have. The need seems urgent, the time short, and your prayers become intense. However, God just keeps moving us forward at His rate of speed, which at times can also seem slow. There is a clear relationship between the magnitude of our problem and the clarity of God's response. The more we want to seek His wisdom for our circumstances, the less He appears to be interested in revealing a quick solution.

After struggling through many long periods of waiting in my life, I have come to understand an important scriptural truth that will free us from considerable bondage and unleash God's power on our behalf. It is the principle of relinquishment, and it leads to one conclusion: God's timing is perfect. He knows when everything is in its proper place and the answer to our situation can be revealed.

He knows all that has to take place in order to meet our need, answer our prayer effectively, and bless us with His goodness. Rushing ahead of Him can be disastrous. In our attempt to take care of the problem or circumstance, we run the risk of missing His best and also stepping outside the boundaries of His will for our lives. Learn to be patient, to wait on God, and to rest in the fact that He is omniscient (all-knowing) and that He would not do anything to harm or frustrate you.

Learning to wait for God's timing is one of the most profitable lessons I have learned. On many occasions, I have petitioned Him for an answer to a need that I felt was pressing, and there has been virtually no response. Did this mean that God was too busy, that He didn't love me, or that I was outside His will? No. God answers prayer in one of three ways: yes, no, and wait. If His answer is yes, then He will open up a way before us that is easy to travel—even when the circumstances are difficult. We will catch ourselves saying, "That was hard, but everything fell into place."

If His answer is no, we will sense this too. If we press Him to answer the way we feel is best, He may just allow us to manipulate our circumstances so we get what we want. When this happens, we are not happy long. Soon, problems come, stresses build, and we wish we had waited for God to work on our behalf.

The third way He answers prayer is by telling us to wait. No matter how long He wants you to remain in one place, be committed to doing it. If He tells you to move forward, then go with a sense of joy in your heart. Never second-guess His goodness, but thank Him for working everything out perfectly in your life.

Letting go of a problem or stressful situation is probably one of the most difficult things we must do. This is especially true when it appears that the answer to our need is right at our fingertips and God doesn't move in that direction. He sees the greater picture. He knows that if we settle for what we think will work, we will miss the greater blessing that He is prepared to send our way.

By relinquishment, I do not mean resignation or passivity. I am not suggesting a mind-set of fatalism or inaction. What I mean is letting go of our demanding spirit, quieting our inner strife, and canceling our own agenda—being completely willing to wait for God's provision.

Jesus is our example. He passionately sought God's will regarding His death: "My Father, if it is possible, let this cup pass from Me; yet not as I will, but as You will" (Matt. 26:39). Because His mission of redemption was incomplete without the cross, Jesus had to surrender His desires to the Father: "Not My will, but Yours be done" (Luke 22:42). It was a prayer of relinquishment, arrived at only after ardent, earnest petition. When Jesus said yes to the Father, Satan's shackles of sin on mankind were shattered. The power that flowed from Calvary is the heart of the Christian faith.

When we submit to God's plan—whatever that may be—we release amazing power within our lives.

Relinquishing a troublesome matter to God means we have placed the situation squarely into the hands of our Lord, whose goodness, wisdom, and power never fail.

Dear heavenly Father, I confess that my thoughts are sometimes off-base with Yours. Right now, I want to give my circumstances to You. With open hands, I lay them before You, not holding on to any part of them. By faith, I am trusting You completely with my needs.

Amen.

No Complaints

I am confident of this very thing, that He who began a good work in you will perfect it until the day of Christ Jesus.
—Phil. 1:6

Some of my fondest memories of childhood are of my mother. My father died when I was nine months old; therefore, my mom supported us for many years. She worked the swing shift at a textile mill, which meant that she came home late each night. We did not have very many worldly possessions, but what we did have could not be taken away from us. We had love—love for one another and most of all love for the Lord. During those early years of my life, we moved several times. In fact, I lived in seventeen houses over a period of sixteen years!

Most people would think that this could lead to my having a sense of instability and hopelessness. This was not the case, however, because my mother was a woman of faith and prayer. She seldom complained and always expressed confidence in the fact that when we trust God to meet our needs, He will prove to be faithful every time. In our household, there was no room for doubt and worry. Sure, there may have been times of great concern, but each instance was an opportunity for us to turn to God and watch Him work on our behalf. Her enthusiasm and faith were contagious, and soon, I grew to trust the Lord with the needs that I had.

In Philippians, Paul tells us, "Do all things without grumbling or disputing" (2:14). Does this seem difficult for you to do when life takes an uncertain turn? If we are honest, when trouble comes, we usually want to cry out, "Lord, why?" It's okay to ask Him to show you why, but it is better to pray, "Lord, help me to understand what You want me to learn in this situation." When we are not bound up in complaining thoughts, our minds are free to hear what He wants us to know about our circumstances.

When I think back to those early years and the many

difficulties I faced as a young man, I am reminded of my mom and how she faced trouble without a hint of murmuring. Her secret is one that you and I can practice each day. She had a thankful heart. This is a principle that every believer can follow successfully. It is found in the verse immediately preceding Paul's command to tackle life with a grateful spirit: "It is God who is at work in you, both to will and to work for His good pleasure" (Phil. 2:13).

Never forget this tremendous truth: God is constantly at work in your life. He is not limited by time, distance, or circumstances, and He is never perplexed by your problems. He is actively moving in your inner being to conform you to Christ's image because He is sovereign (over all things), and He is engineering the circumstances of your life so that you can experience His full blessing and also so that He may be glorified.

We can genuinely give thanks in everything (1 Thess. 5:18) because God is at work in all things. Why grumble or complain if God is in control and accomplishing His purposes? I am convinced that it was because my mother understood this principle that she was able to go about her duties with a grateful heart.

Do you see God at work in your life? If so, then each assignment of the day—great or small—bears His imprint. Refuse to yield to a critical or complaining spirit, because to do so is actually to grumble against God Himself (Ex. 16:8). But a thankful spirit promotes peace and health. It acknowledges God's love and affirms your trust in Him. It is a solid testimony to others that the God you serve is able, caring, and very wise.

God, forgive me for grumbling and complaining about so many things. There is so much to be thankful for. I know a grateful heart promotes peace, and that is what I want. I give You permission to change my critical spirit and replace it with thanksgiving.

Amen.

WALKING IN LOVE

Therefore as you have received Christ Jesus the Lord,
so walk in Him.
—Col. 2:6)

The authors of the New Testament frequently wrote about the "Christian walk" as a description of believers' behavior. For example, we are told to walk as children of light, walk in the truth, walk according to the Spirit, and walk in love. In Colossians 2:6, Paul uses this expression to give us an important command: "Therefore as you have received Christ Jesus the Lord, so walk in Him." The question we must ask is, what does it mean to "walk in Christ"?

Here, the word *in* does not have a literal usage like "the hammer is in the toolbox." Rather, it refers to a vital relationship—a union between the believer and the Lord. Just as a wedding marks the beginning of a new relationship for a husband and a wife, receiving Christ as your Savior marks the beginning of an intimate and personal relationship between you and God.

He forgives your sin and also sets the groundwork in place to develop a close and ever-deepening relationship with you. He wants you to realize that the Son of God is your constant Companion—your Source for every need you have.

Therefore, "walking in Christ" refers to a dynamic relationship with the Lord. Just as it is impossible to walk while standing still, believers are either moving forward in their Christian life or falling backward. The key to making progress is found in that same verse, Colossians 2:6: "As you have received Christ Jesus the Lord, so walk in Him." How did you and I receive Christ? By faith. In order to be born again, we trusted the testimony of the Word of God. The Christian life is to be "walked"—or lived out—in the same way.

We often are tempted to trust our feelings instead of asking God to lead and guide us. No wonder we make a mess of things at times. He sees the beginning of our lives along with the ending. He knows when we will take a wrong turn, but He is also aware of the many moments when we will turn to Him for help. This is when He moves quickly on our behalf—not just to meet our physical needs, but our mental, emotional, and spiritual needs as well.

Once a young man told me, "I have made a horrible mistake. There is no way God can love me or ever use me again." This just is not true. God knows exactly how to mend and then use broken lives. There may be unavoidable consequences to the sin, but once we confess that what we have done is wrong, God moves quickly to embrace us and restore us for His glory.

The enemy, however, wants to destroy our witness for Christ. He tempts us and then accuses us when we fall for his lies. But God never leaves, always forgives, and promises to love us with an everlasting love. How does God want us to live each day? Paul instructs that the followers of Jesus Christ are to "walk by faith, not by sight" (2 Cor. 5:7). It is the love of God that teaches us exactly how to do this.

We must take the first step by faith, and then another,

not knowing exactly where our footfalls will take us but trusting that our omniscient, loving God has our best interest in mind. To walk in faith means having a personal relationship with Jesus Christ that results in trusting Him in every circumstance of life. When we consistently live with that kind of confidence in the Lord, we will believe He will do what is right and what is for our benefit every time, without exception.

Dear Father, it is difficult to trust when the hardships of life seem so many. Yet I know that in trusting You, I will not only see the victory over adversity but will grow closer to You. Please help me to trust You more and, in doing so, to know You more.

Amen.

LOVE'S FIRST PROMISE

"You have left your first love."
—Rev. 2:4

What happens when you feel a sudden pain of rejection? Maybe you did not see it coming, and before you could brace yourself, a friend or loved one withdrew their love. Some writers have described it as an emptiness of heart. If you have ever experienced this, you know exactly what it feels like. A sunny day seems dark and unsettling. Tears come without warning. There is an uncomfortable feeling in all that you do, and you find yourself praying that love will return. Somehow, you expect to open the door and find your loved one there, and everything will be fine once again.

In Revelation 2, Jesus is talking about the various churches located throughout the world. He mentions the church in Ephesus and makes this unsettling comment: "I know your deeds and your toil and perseverance, and that you cannot tolerate evil men . . . and you have perseverance and have endured for My name's sake, and have not grown weary. But I have this against you, that you have left your first love" (vv. 2–4).

There are times when we walk away from God— leaving Him in sorrow. This is what it means to leave your first love. Even though you are going through the motions, your heart is not drawn to Him in love. Your affections are on something or someone else.

Is your relationship with Jesus your first priority? Or have you become so preoccupied with the trappings of this world that you no longer have time for the commitment of a personal relationship with Him?

If you think you may have hit a plateau in your fellowship with Christ, consider these questions: Is He still your "first love"? Do you enjoy spending time with Him? Do you tell others about what He is teaching you? Do you begrudge giving a tithe of your income? Your responses to questions like these could reveal the quality of your friendship with the Savior. Knowing Him as your first love means you are increasingly excited about knowing Him—His ways and His Word. The church at Ephesus had drifted away from its original devotion to the Savior, but this does not have to be true of your life.

Activity, though essential to practical faith, is not a substitute for personal fellowship. It can never outweigh intimacy with God. Many times, busyness can prevent us from focusing on God's love and goodness. Also, the gods of this age—entertainment, work, and money—while not bad in and of themselves, can too often become substitutes for our devotion to God. Immoral relationships can leave us feeling guilty and questioning God's love and acceptance. Instead of enjoying His fellowship, we end up wondering if our sin has caused Him to turn away from us. He never does, but when our heart's devotion is focused on something or someone other than Him, we will sense a distance growing between Him and us. Has He moved? No, but we have.

How can you recapture that first love? Remember

what Christ did for you on the cross: the supernatural transformation that took you from death to life, from darkness to light, from the dominion of sin to the reign of Christ. Repent of whatever has diminished your love for the Savior. Make a commitment to turn away from the things that are distracting you, and begin to spend time in prayer and fellowship with Him. Ask Him to give you a love for His Word, and study it with the single purpose of encountering God.

As a young Christian, I was introduced to the writings of Oswald Chambers, who put his relationship with Christ above all else. In his book *The Moral Foundations of Life,* Chambers writes, "Never allow anything to fuss your relationship to Jesus Christ, neither Christian work, nor Christian blessing, nor Christian anything. Jesus Christ first, second, and third, and God Himself by the great indwelling power of the Spirit within, will meet the strenuous effort on your part and slowly and surely you will form the mind of Christ and become one with Him as He was one with the Father."

Dear Lord, it's easy to take Your love for granted, to become so preoccupied with the business of everyday life that I spend less and less time with You. Yet I know the time I spend in fellowship with You should be the most important part of my day. Please teach me to place You first in my life and to guard the time I have with You as being sacred.

Amen.

AN ENCOURAGING WORD

[Paul] traveled through that area,
speaking many words of encouragement to the people.
—*Acts 20:2 NIV*

Have you ever been encouraged or inspired by the words of a close friend? Most of us have. We find ourselves struggling with a crucial decision or a disappointment, and suddenly, someone says something that causes us to think about God's goodness. The Lord tells us in Jeremiah 29:11, "I know the plans that I have for you . . . plans for welfare and not for calamity to give you a future and a hope."

You are always on God's mind. There is never a moment when He fails to think about you. Many people make the mistake of thinking that His thoughts toward them are ones of displeasure, but this is not true. When He sees your life, He sees potential, hope, and a person

He loves unconditionally. This is why He inspired the prophet Jeremiah to write, "plans for welfare and not for calamity to give you a future and a hope." God has a plan for your future, and it is one of promise and blessing, but you must be willing to submit yourself to Him—His counsel, His timing, and His purpose. When you do this, you will know true joy.

I can still remember a time long ago when this happened to me—I was only six years old. On that day, as I was leaving my school room, I overheard my teacher comment to another, "I like Charles." It was the first time a person other than my mom had ever said they liked me, and I suddenly felt like I was walking on air. My teacher's three simple words were emotional fuel that boosted my confidence and even changed the way I viewed myself.

Have you ever thought how influential your words are? Do you know what kind of impact your speech can have on a person who desperately needs to hear an encouraging word? Solomon writes, "Pleasant words are a honeycomb, sweet to the soul and healing to the bones" (Prov. 16:24). What a wonderful way to describe our conversation. It can be medicine to a weary soul, healing to a bruised spirit. Kind words, spoken in due season, are God's bridges of love.

If you've been on the receiving end of gracious comments, you know the power of well-chosen words. Perhaps a coach noticed you at practice one day and remarked how well you had performed. Or maybe a coworker came to you and commended your work and attitude on a difficult task. Paul describes such speech as being "with grace, as though seasoned with salt" (Col. 4:6). Our remarks, he says, are to be flavored with gentleness and lovingkindness—the key ingredients of grace-filled speech.

The love of Christ can transform our speech if we allow Him to work in our lives. When your words reflect His love and compassion, you will see a profound change in your relationships.

Ask God to make you aware of the needs of others. When we are completely absorbed in our own problems or activities, complimentary words rarely grace our conversation. But when our focus is on edification rather than condemnation, our speech can be used for "edification according to the need of the moment, so that it will give grace to those who hear" (Eph. 4:29).

Heavenly Father, speak words of encouragement through me. Help me to take my focus off of my own problems, and make me sensitive to the needs of others.

Amen.

OUR GREATEST PRIVILEGE

May the Lord direct your hearts into the love of God.
—2 Thess. 3:5

Of all the people you have met, whom do you feel most privileged to know? Is it an athlete or an accomplished performer? Perhaps it is an admired coworker, a precious grandparent, a godly mother or father, or a friend. As special as these people may be, our supreme privilege is to know God.

A personal, intimate relationship with Jesus Christ is an unparalleled opportunity and eternal treasure. Nothing else in human existence—no experience, friendship, or knowledge—can bring you lasting peace, joy, fulfillment, or security. Nothing else offers eternal life.

The apostle Paul recognized that even the most highly esteemed achievements pale in comparison to the "surpassing value of knowing Christ" (Phil. 3:8). In fact, his consuming desire was to know the Savior—the One who had transformed his very being. In contrast, many people go through life without ever knowing Him. They reach the end of their days as unbelievers, failing to discover the purpose for which they were created and missing the blessings of God. This is a great tragedy!

Why do people bypass the opportunity to have a personal relationship with Jesus Christ? To begin with, many have chosen to live in spiritual darkness. They are unaware of the saving grace and unconditional love of God. Perhaps they were never exposed to Christian truth, which can happen within churches that have adopted a liberal view of the gospel message and no longer emphasize salvation as a way to know Christ and gain eternal life.

Another reason people lack interest in the Lord is because they are too busy. Computers, cell phones, radios, televisions, and after-school and work activities keep us emotionally and physically tied up. We are overwhelmed by the amount of information we receive each day, and we are no wiser because of it. Convinced that access to information equals knowledge, we often replace the wisdom of God with simple trivia. Diplomas may cover your walls, but unless you know Jesus Christ as your personal Savior, you are ignorant about the most important thing in life—and that is God's redemptive love for you.

Knowing God requires a commitment. A cost is involved, but the payout has the best return in the universe. Far too often, people accept Christ as their Savior and then become satisfied and idle in their relationship with Him. They are not interested in investing time in Scripture and prayer to know the Father more deeply. For any relationship to grow, we must spend time talking, listening, and making an effort to understand more about the other person. This is especially true of our relationship with the Lord.

Do you really want to know God? The way to do that is by knowing Christ. Receive Him as your Savior, the One who paid your sin debt in full. Then accept His invitation to spend time in private conversation—He wants your undivided attention.

Lord, I do love You. I may not know exactly how to express my love, but I know I can count on You to instruct me through your Word. I ask, Lord, that You will supernaturally empower me to love others as Christ loves them. Guard my intentions, that they will not be misunderstood. Let others see Jesus, not me.

Amen.

LOVE IN ACTION

"A new commandment I give to you, that you love one another,
even as I have loved you, that you also love one another.
By this all men will know that you are My disciples."
—John 13:34–35

When I was growing up, Craig Stowe was my Sunday school teacher. But I remember him for something much more than the way he taught my class. He often stopped me on the street while I was on my paper route to purchase a newspaper from me. He would spend five or ten minutes just talking with me, asking me about my family, school, and things that matter to a young boy. Not only that, he always gave me more than what the newspaper cost. It didn't take me long to figure out that he did not need to buy a newspaper—he got the newspaper at home. He was interested in me, and his actions—that continued for several years of my young life—demonstrated God's love to me.

He went out of his way to show that he wasn't just my Sunday school teacher. He involved himself in my life, and I will never forget him. Kind words are important, but kind deeds also exhibit the love of Christ in a tangible way. Jesus did not just say He loves us; He demonstrated His love by dying for our sins (Rom. 5:8).

Before His death, Jesus told His disciples that the world would know they were His followers by showing their love for one another (John 13:35). He obviously meant they would live in a way that visibly and practically expressed God's love. This is His commandment to each one of us today. His Word has not changed because He knows the value of godly love expressed through words and deeds that encourage and bring a fresh sense of hope to those who are tired, lonely, alone, overwhelmed, and feeling rejected.

Barnabas encouraged a downcast young man named Mark, who later penned one of the Gospels. Mary and Martha showed their love for Christ by inviting Him to dine and rest in their home in Bethany. Paul reminded Titus that Christ's death not only saved us from sin but also should motivate us to be "zealous [to do] good deeds" (Titus 2:14). We were "created in Christ Jesus for good works" (Eph. 2:10).

By treating others the way Christ treats us—with love, compassion, and forgiveness—we proclaim the message of the gospel without saying a word. The next time God reminds you that a neighbor could be lonely, bake a pie or some cookies for her and her family. Take time to mow the yard for an elderly person; invite a widowed friend out to lunch; take a coffee break with a frustrated coworker; help a new neighbor unload the boxes that are still in his garage; or write an encouraging note to someone who just needs to hear the words, "Thank you" or "I'm grateful to know you."

Sharing God's love in this manner reveals the personal compassion of Christ and says "I care" louder than any words possibly could. All it requires is a willingness to be used by God to encourage someone else. Take a moment and ask Him who in your life needs a touch of His love and hope today.

Lord, I worry about my own problems so much that I forget that others around me have needs as well. Show me how to demonstrate Your love and concern to others. Thank You for the many times others have gone out of their way to show me special attention. Help me to act when I see someone with a need that I can meet.

Amen.

WHEN WE PRAISE

I will bow down toward Your holy temple and give thanks to Your
name for Your lovingkindness and Your truth.
—Ps. 138:2

The more you love God, the more you will want to worship Him. This is because love and praise are natural partners. Heaven is a place where those who love God live in constant praise of Him. However, should life lived here on earth be any different? We praise God not only for what He has done for us but for who He is—the God of the universe—all-powerful, all-knowing, compassionate, long-suffering, and totally committed to each one of us.

"Praise Him for His mighty deeds," writes the psalmist in Psalm 150:2. His "mighty deeds" are the extraordinary events recorded in Scripture—creation, miracles, the cross, and the resurrection. These also are the remarkable displays of His personal love for you. Why not write down some of the ways that God has demonstrated His power in your life? Think of His guidance, His provision, His protection, and the numerous other ways He has supplied your personal needs. Keeping a journal that records God's work in your life is a tremendous tool for joyful praise and helps you recall His faithfulness.

We praise Him for "His excellent greatness" (Ps. 150:2). This is pure praise, standing in awe of God for who He is. He is faithful, kind, good, just, holy, patient, and generous. The Lord is quick to act on our behalf because He loves us, and He is our Protector and Redeemer. His character and attributes should overwhelm us with a desire to bow down before Him in adoration and praise. Our response should be nothing short of ecstatic gratitude. Think of this: you have the opportunity to worship God, the One who loves you with a love that will never fade.

Praise magnifies God and puts our problems in proper perspective. We often worry about our circumstances instead of taking each issue to God in prayer and leaving it in His capable hands. What obstacle is too great for Him to handle? What circumstance is too difficult? Many times, I have gone to the Lord in prayer over a burden that was too difficult for me to solve. God is our burden bearer (Ps. 55:22).

In Psalm 68:19, the psalmist writes, "Blessed be the Lord, who daily bears our burden, the God who is our salvation." He cares so much about you that He carries—bears the weight of—every burden you have. If there is a need, He always provides a solution.

Prayer, along with praise and worship, reveals our true devotion to Christ. Habakkuk the prophet was committed to praising God even in the worst of times. "Though the fig tree should not blossom and there be no fruit on the vines, though the yield of the olive should fail and the fields produce no food, though the flock should be cut off from the fold and there be no cattle in the stalls, yet I will exult in the LORD, I will rejoice in the God of my salvation" (Hab. 3:17–18).

Even if your circumstances are dismal and there appears to be no immediate hope, God deserves your praise. This is exactly what David discovered and what he practiced. In Psalm 18, he wrote, "I call upon the LORD, who is worthy to be praised, and I am saved from my enemies" (v. 3). Faith in an unshakable God and praise are the very stepping-stones that lead you away from the feelings of depression and discouragement. When you praise Him, something within you changes. You gain a new perspective—His perspective—and it is one of hope and potential. Joy comes no matter how dark the night may appear. Fears vanish in the presence of His glory, and you are drawn even nearer to Him.

Therefore, enter His presence with a thankful heart as you present your request to Him. Choose to praise Him in difficult times—it makes all the difference. "Shout joyfully to the LORD, all the earth . . . come before Him with joyful singing" (Ps. 100:1–2).

Heavenly Father, I do want to praise You. I do not want to dwell on my problems and needs but only on all You have done for me. Your Word tells me that from the very beginning of time, You had a plan for my life, desiring for me to accept Your Son as my Savior. You have watched over me and directed my life for my good and Your glory. Thank You for all You have done for me.

Amen.

MORE THAN A FEELING

No one will snatch them out of My hand.
—John 10:28

Sir Winston Churchill once remarked that it was dangerous to "always [be] feeling one's pulse and taking one's temperature." His words were addressed to those who looked at the wildly fluctuating fortunes of battles to determine England's success or failure in World War II.

His words also are applicable to Christians who constantly gauge their relationship with Christ by their feelings. Emotions are unreliable barometers, and if you attach your faith to them, you will, without a doubt, be misguided. There are times when the Bible may seem cold to us—when our prayers feel listless, and our commitment to the church uncertain. If we allow our feelings to govern our fellowship with Christ in times like these, we will be tempted to fall into feelings of guilt and self-condemnation.

The Bible teaches us, "Love the Lord your God with all your heart, and with all your soul, and with all your strength, and with all your mind" (Luke 10:27), but what do you do when you have waited for God to answer a sincere prayer and He has not responded? Do you give up? No. Do you listen to the enemy of your soul who is quick to remind you that you still do not know what is right for you to do? Absolutely not! You wait, trusting the One who is invisible to our human eyes but alive within our hearts.

We trust with hearts that are devoted to God because He has an incredible love for us. The prescription for a steady, progressive walk of faith is learning to focus on Christ rather than our circumstances. Circumstances change, feelings are not stable, but God remains the same—yesterday, today, and forever.

Imagine your hand being clasped together with God's. Even though you may loosen your grip as a result of temptation, sin, doubt, or apathy, God will never let go of you. Your feelings of love for Him may fade, but His love for you never does. It remains solid. "Your right hand upholds me," declared David from the deserts of Judah (Ps. 63:8). "I am the LORD, your God, who upholds your right hand," said God to a fearful people (Isa. 41:13).

You are eternally secure in the love of God because love to Him is much more than a feeling. Once you accept His Son as your Savior, He seals your life by the power and presence of the Holy Spirit, and heaven awaits you. In this light, you can cease exercising self-centered faith. You can stop measuring the depth of your love for Christ by inconsistent feelings and instead base your faith on the unwavering love of God.

Heavenly Father, I can be so easily influenced by my feelings, and the results of my actions can be devastating. Strengthen my faith in You. My heart's desire is to grasp Your hand firmly at all times. Teach me to overcome feelings that are damaging to my faith. Thank You, Father, for Your steadfast love.

Amen.

TRUE LOVE GIVES

God loves a cheerful giver.
—2 Cor. 9:7

A scriptural synonym for "love" is the word *give*. "God so loved the world, that He *gave* His only begotten Son" (John 3:16, emphasis added). "I live by faith in the Son of God, who loved me and *gave* Himself up for me" (Gal. 2:20, emphasis added).

God gives us the gift of salvation and the Holy Spirit. He also gives His peace, strength, and wisdom to those who ask. It is impossible to love someone without giving something of yourself away.

We bestow our affection on family members and friends with various forms of giving. We demonstrate our commitment to Christ and others by giving our time, our resources, and our energies. Generosity is a true hallmark of genuine Christianity. Proverbs 11:25

says, "The generous man will be prosperous, and he who waters will himself be watered." Giving is the channel through which the love of God flows.

I remember as a young man how we had very little. However, my mother always made sure that there was enough for us to eat in the refrigerator and something extra for anyone who happened to drop by our home. Many times, I watched her gather a few things together to give to someone she knew was hungry and had less than we did. Once or twice I even thought, *Mom, if you give that away, we won't have enough*, but we always did. She lived by faith and taught me to do the same. Consequently, we were never without, and I believe it was because my mother knew the principle of giving regardless of sacrifice.

You may think you have too little to give, but whatever your financial or physical situation, there is always something you can offer others. If you wait until you have a surplus to give, you will never begin. A generous person demonstrates God's love by giving even the little things—a listening ear, a tip for the grocery boy, a handmade gift for Christmas.

Have you ever noticed that people are drawn to a generous person, not for a handout but because of the inviting spiritual atmosphere that surrounds him? A generous person is sensitive to the needs of others and gives from the heart, not for the purpose of receiving something in return. He derives joy in seeing others benefit from his benevolence. He views needs as an opportunity, not a threat. He wants to see how much he can give, not how little. He trusts God for his own needs.

Why is giving so important? Because it is the certain cure for greed. God blesses generosity and curses greed. Giving is the antidote for selfishness, a lifestyle that does not reflect the likeness of Christ. Generosity also opens the heart of both the giver and receiver to the love of Christ. You can't be a giver without learning how to receive. Both can become spiritually prosperous by exercising the important principle of giving. Some people love to give, but they are uncomfortable receiving anything from someone else. Usually, this is the result of deep-seated pride. God not only wants us to be cheerful givers, but also to be cheerful as we receive good gifts from Him and gifts of love from those around us.

If you are reluctant to give, stingy with your resources, and isolated from the needs of others, you are missing out on fantastic blessings from your generous heavenly Father. "Give, and it will be given to you," Jesus promised (Luke 6:38). Such is the power of generosity. Give something today, and watch God work. Better yet, accept His precious gift of love, and you will be changed forever!

Lord, please show me a way that I can give of myself to benefit others and glorify You. I know there are many people around me who are hurting and in need of a kind word spoken to them. Teach me to be sensitive to those who are lonely and need encouragement.

Amen.

WILLING TO SAY YES

Christ's love compels us.
—2 Cor. 5:14 NIV

The Lord's simple requests are often doorways to life's most wonderful blessings. Simon Peter is a good illustration of what happens when we say yes to God. In Luke 5:1–11, people were pressing in around Jesus while He was preaching. Therefore, the Lord asked if He could get into Peter's boat and speak to the crowd on the shore. In fact, the Savior even asked the burly fisherman to push his boat away from the shoreline in order for the people to hear what was being said (v. 3). This in and of itself was not a particularly remarkable request. However, Peter's compliance was, and it paved the way for a much greater blessing. Obedience to God is essential no matter how small the request may seem.

Immediately, the crowd was blessed by Peter's obedience—they were able to hear Christ's words as He taught the Word of God. When Jesus concluded His teaching, He turned to Peter and made an even stranger request: "Put out into the deep water and let down your nets for a catch" (v. 4). Peter, along with John and the others, had been fishing all night, and they had caught nothing. The reason they were still near the water's edge was because they were cleaning their nets in preparation for the following evening, when they would return to the shallow waters to fish.

No one fishes on the Sea of Galilee in the heat of the day, and especially in deep water. Peter knew this, but he also recognized that Jesus was much more than an ordinary teacher from a local synagogue. Here was another opportunity for Peter to say yes or no.

Obedience is critical to our walk with God. Suppose Peter had said, "I'm too busy cleaning my nets right now. I can't help You because I'm going fishing again tonight—I just don't have time." Or he could have said,

"Why don't You use another boat?" Or "I've already been fishing today. It would be a waste of time to go again right now." Peter could have listed a number of reasons why he did not want to go back out on the Sea of Galilee. If he had said anything other than yes, he would have missed the greatest fishing experience of his life. Because of Peter's obedience, the Lord arranged a miracle he would never forget. On a day that he and his colleagues had written off as a total loss, they pulled in not one but two overflowing boatloads of fish (v. 7). Saying yes to the Lord's request resulted in a miracle that absolutely transformed Peter's life.

Oftentimes God's greatest blessings come as a result of our willingness to do something that appears to be very insignificant. Has God been challenging you to do something seemingly unimportant that you have not yet made an effort to accomplish? Is there anything you have rationalized by saying, "It's too difficult," "I don't want to," or "I have to pray about it"? Obey God today, and receive His full blessing.

Dear God, it is easy to serve You out of a sense of duty rather than love. I love You, Lord, because You first loved me. I want to serve You—not from a place of fear but out of love and devotion. Help me to discern the difference so I may be used effectively by You.

Amen.

A FATHER'S LOVE

Your lovingkindness toward me is great.
—Ps. 86:13

I remember coming home one day from the church, and as I walked past the car my daughter usually drove, I noticed the front end had been damaged. After hearing that she was okay, I asked her what had happened. She explained that she was traveling along one of the major expressways in Atlanta when suddenly, the cars in front of her came to a complete stop. She applied the brakes, but it was too late. Her car slid straight into the back of the one in front of her.

When she got to this point in the story, her eyes filled with tears, and she said, "Dad, I'm sorry that I wrecked the car." Immediately, I was overcome with emotion. The thought of anything happening to her was far too much for me to grasp. I wasn't worried about the car. Cars can be replaced, but daughters cannot. As I hugged her, I realized how precious she was to me.

When things go wrong in life and we end up hurting, our heavenly Father reaches out and gathers us into His loving arms of grace and mercy. He's not worried about the loss of things. His only concern is for us—His beloved children. He is the God who cares deeply for us—the Father who loves us with an endless, abiding love.

When you pray, how do you address Him? Without a doubt, the greatest privilege we have is to call Him our Father. In fact, Jesus taught His disciples to pray this way, "Our Father who is in heaven" (Matt. 6:9).

The possibility of having such a close relationship with God was a revolutionary concept in the first century. The Old Testament contains only fifteen references to God as "Father," and those speak primarily of Him as the father of the Hebrew people; the idea of His being a personal God to individuals is not evident until the New Testament. Yet that is the reason Jesus Christ came to earth—to die on the cross for our sins and reveal the heavenly Father so that you and I might know Him intimately.

"Father," which appears 245 times in the New Testament, was Jesus' favorite name for God. He spoke it fourteen times in the Sermon on the Mount and also used this name to begin His prayers. Christ's purpose was to teach us a powerful truth: God is a loving, personal, heavenly Father who is completely interested in every detail of our lives. Someone reading these words may have never experienced a father's love. God understands, and He is willing to take your emptiness, brokenness, and all your hurts and mend each one.

The privilege of knowing God as Father involves more than being familiar with Him as the God of the Bible. It goes far beyond simple familiarity with His matchless grace, love, and kindness, and even surpasses knowing Him in His holiness, righteousness, and justice. The relationship that God has with each one of us as His children is a bond of love that cannot be broken.

By addressing Him as "Father," Jesus revealed the depth of His own relationship with God. This is something the saints of the Old Testament could not fully grasp. We have the blessing of intimate kinship with the living God of the universe. In fact, it is through the person of Jesus Christ that we are able to know God in this way. We can sit with Him, worship Him, open our hearts up to Him, and know that we always will be accepted because we are His.

Do you know God loves you more than anyone could ever love you? He stands ready to adopt you into His family (Rom. 8:15; Gal. 3:26). All it takes is to trust His Son, Jesus Christ, as your personal Savior. As John 1:12 says, "As many as received Him, to them He gave the right to become children of God, even to those who believe in His name."

Dear Father, it's good to know I have such an intimate friend as You. Because of Your omnipotence, I can trust You to lead me through the dark shadows of life. I know You will always be right beside me. Thank You, my dear Father.

Amen.

LOVE'S PROMISE

There is no fear in love; but perfect love casts out fear.
—1 John 4:18

Doctors, psychologists, and counselors tell us that one of the things people want most is to be loved. Following close behind is a need to be accepted, and in many cases, people will go to great lengths to gain the approval of others. The result of this quest has left us fighting an intense battle with feelings of loneliness and fear—fear that no one will love us, and loneliness from the isolation that comes from striving after something we were never created to seek.

When we struggle for the approval of others, we bypass the unconditional acceptance of God. We may think, *Oh, I know God loves me*, but essentially we are saying His love is not good enough, and we need the love of others in order to feel needed and wanted. Jesus told His disciples to seek the kingdom of God first and then all their needs would be met (Matt. 6:33).

When the focus of our heart is placed squarely on God, every need, every desire we have is fulfilled. This places us in a right relationship with God, which is a place of abiding peace that comes from His presence within us through the power of the Holy Spirit. God loves us regardless of the bumps, bruises, and emotional scars we have collected. He cares when we hurt and when we suffer discouragement. He is our eternal Friend. Only God has the capacity to show such incredible love and acceptance.

Jesus took great care to assure His disciples that His impending death was not the end of God's presence on earth. A Comforter, One who possessed the same characteristics as He did, would come. Jesus said, "I will ask the Father, and He will give you another Helper . . . that is the Spirit of truth, whom the world cannot receive, because it does not see Him or know Him, but you know

Him because He abides with you and will be in you. I will not leave you as orphans; I will come to you" (John 14:16–18).

Lasting relationships always require good communication and trust. Jesus made an eternal pledge when He came to earth. To realize the completeness of God's fellowship, we must make a commitment to Him.

The essence of the Christian life does not consist of a set of rules and regulations. It is sharing a moment-by-moment, intimate relationship with the Savior. It is not a matter of human acceptance. God accepts us—that is all we need.

Friendship with the Savior is a continuous unveiling of His love and personal care for each of us. The life that remains focused on Jesus Christ is a life that enjoys unbroken fellowship. It is a life of victory, peace, hope, security, and, most of all, friendship.

Dear heavenly Father, Your love is never–ending, and Your protection is always present. Please help me to focus on the love of Christ as I go through my day, and cause that love to overflow into my other relationships.

Amen.

TOUGH LOVE

Those whom I love, I reprove and discipline;
therefore be zealous and repent.
—Rev. 3:19

Cloth can be used to dust off a piece of gold, but for embedded impurities to be removed, the metal must be refined. In other words, it must be melted by fire so that any tarnish or flaw can rise and be skimmed from the surface.

The godly life is often compared to this process (Mal. 3:3). When you face struggles, God is refining you like this precious metal. He is digging deep into your life to eliminate all the dirt and impurities that prevent you from knowing Him and glorifying His name. He does not do this to hurt you, but rather to help you grow into a beautiful reflection of His Son. Brokenness at the hand of God also leads to tremendous blessing. If you are going through a particularly hard time, you can be assured that God has something much better in store for you.

David endured many trials. Some of these were due to his waywardness. Others were opportunities for God to strengthen him and prepare him for a greater work. In Psalm 18 he wrote, "Who is God, but the LORD? And who is a rock, except our God, the God who girds me with strength and makes my way blameless? He makes my feet like hinds' feet, and sets me upon my high places. He trains my hands for battle, so that my arms can bend a bow of bronze. You have also given me the shield of Your salvation, and Your right hand upholds me; and Your gentleness makes me great. You enlarge my steps under me, and my feet have not slipped" (vv. 31–36).

God is always in the process of shaping and molding your life in order to use you for His glory and to bless you in a mighty way. David learned that while the Lord's rebuke may have seemed harsh momentarily, it was necessary for his growth and future. Athletes who refuse to train for their sport are rarely outstanding. However, those who excel spend countless hours in training, going over and over a single motion. They also build up their body strength through rigorous exercise until they are prepared for the event in which they will compete.

God's discipline is always motivated by love. "Those whom the Lord loves He disciplines" (Heb. 12:6). Therefore, when difficulty comes, refuse to fall into feelings of self-pity. Ask the Lord to show you why He has allowed the problem or sorrow to come. Also, pray that He will use this in your life to draw you even closer to Him. Keep in mind that some sorrows are unavoidable. The sudden death of a loved one can leave us grasping for hope and understanding. God knows when you are hurting, and if you will turn to Him, He will carry you through the deepest of emotional valleys.

The author of Hebrews reminds us, "It is for discipline that you endure; God deals with you as with sons" (12:7). You are God's beloved child. Never mistake His discipline for anger or feel as though your relationship with Him has cruelly changed when adversity strikes. You have been adopted into His family, and discipline only enables you to enjoy fully the benefits of His fatherhood.

"He disciplines us for our good, so that we may share His holiness" (Heb. 12:10). The pain of chastisement has a purpose—to conform us to the image of Jesus Christ. Therefore, do not turn away or become bitter when life becomes stormy. Remember, God allows difficulty so that we will learn to trust Him to a greater degree. He wants you to run to Him in times of heartache and peril, and anything that drives you to Him is good for you.

My loving Father, the struggles of this life are difficult and often hard to understand. Yet I know that as I endure each trial, You are there with me. Furthermore, I know that You have a purpose in every hardship. As much as I don't like to be disciplined, I am very grateful that You love me enough to intervene in my life in this way.

Amen.

FAITHFUL PROMISES

He has granted to us His precious and magnificent promises.
—2 Peter 1:4

God is always faithful. And if you will allow Him to work in your life, you will witness His faithfulness in dramatic ways. At a crucial point in my life and in the life of the church I pastor, God used the following verse to remind me that He was working mightily: "You are the God who works wonders; You have made known Your strength among the peoples" (Ps. 77:14).

I remember meditating on this verse daily for weeks. I also applied it to the problem I was facing. While I may not have been sure of the earthly outcome, I was certain God was in control and at work—bringing everything together His way and in His time (Rom. 8:28). Sure enough, as I placed my trust in the Lord and as my congregation followed in the same footsteps of faith, God not only intervened—He blessed us with a supernatural answer to prayer.

You, too, can rely on the promises of God's Word. The Bible is a book of principles as well as promises. It is full of verses that teach us of God's intention to graciously bestow good gifts on His children. Some promises are conditional; God will act in a certain way if you obey a certain command, as in, "Give, and it will be given to you" (Luke 6:38). Others are unconditional, given to His children regardless of what they do, such as Isaiah 54:10: "For the mountains may be removed and the hills may shake, but My lovingkindness will not removed from you, and My covenant of peace will not be shaken." The Lord has given us thousands of promises within His Word that He wants us to claim for the circumstances that we face each day.

Bible promises are God's declaration of His love for us. They remind us that He has assumed full responsibility for meeting our needs. For example, if we are struggling with feelings of anxiety, we can claim the following verses as God's promise and provision: "Be anxious for nothing, but in everything by prayer and supplication with thanksgiving let your requests be made known to God. And the peace of God, which surpasses all comprehension, will guard your hearts and your minds in Christ Jesus" (Phil. 4:6–7) and "Cease striving and know that I am God" (Ps. 46:10).

You can be certain that God will fulfill all of His promises, but you must learn to be patient and wait for His deliverance. Remember, He operates according to His time schedule—not yours. He also sees the end from the beginning and knows precisely when to act. Therefore, do not lose heart or become discouraged in the process. It may take days, months, or even years for the promise to bear fruit, but God will keep His word. Remain focused on God's Word, letting Him speak to you specifically through Scripture. Be obedient in your daily trials, yielded and submitted to the revealed will of God.

God's promises are anchors for your soul. They keep you grounded in His love and faithfulness, reminding you of your dependence on Him. What God promises, He will fulfill. As David Livingstone, the noted missionary, said, "It is the word of a Gentleman of the most sacred and strictest honour, and there's an end on it!" Claim it as your own, and stand in faith until God replies.

Thank You, Lord, for standing behind Your promises. They are reliable and trustworthy and for me. Your Word is truth, and I can always count on that when the need is great. Help me to learn Your promises that apply to my circumstances and to stand firmly in You.

Amen.

WAITING ON THE LORD

*Jacob served seven years for Rachel and they seemed to him
but a few days because of his love for her.*
—Gen. 29:20

It can take an entire day for me to photograph an
image—waiting for the right light, framing the shot
exactly, properly checking for the right exposure, and so
on. However, those outings never seem long or tedious
because of my love for photography. In fact, the old adage
is right: "Time flies when you are having fun"—when
you love what you are doing and are excited about the
results.

Do you love what you do each day, or does your
work or life feel more like a frustrating labor rather than
something that is challenging and fulfilling? Is your heart
content, having the "continual feast" of happiness that
Proverbs 15:15 describes? Or is it weighed down with

anxiety or boredom? Regardless of sadness or hardship, God will transform your attitude so you can approach every task and relationship with a cheerful disposition.

Jim Elliot, a missionary who was martyred in Ecuador, said, "Wherever you are, be all there." You may want to be in another job, another marriage, another state, or another home; but the key to enjoying life is contentment with your present situation, as difficult as that may be. Ask God to give you His contentment and to help you live with a sense of unshakable peace because He is your Savior and the Lord over all things.

"Godliness actually is a means of great gain when accompanied by contentment" (1 Tim. 6:6). While it is good to dream and set goals for the future, it also is wise to live each day enjoying what God has given you. He never makes a mistake, and if He is allowing you to be in a narrow place, then you can be assured that it is for a purpose. Instead of dreading each day, begin to focus your energy on making the most of where God has placed you. You will be amazed at the joy and fulfillment that you will experience. Also, take time to enjoy small moments—times that could seem insignificant often have the greatest impact.

The author of Ecclesiastes tells us, "Every man who eats and drinks sees good in all his labor—it is the gift of God" (3:13). Your life is a gift from God, whatever your situation. Even in strenuous seasons, we can discover deep inner peace through knowing Christ. When you face the testing of hardship, remember that God has orchestrated your life according to His perfect will. Your circumstances may not always be wrapped in pretty packages, but the loving hand of God—for your good— gives them. The joy of the Lord really can become your strength (Neh. 8:10).

With God's help, you can learn to love what you do, enjoy where you are, and be satisfied with your relationships. When that happens, then—as with Jacob—the years will seem like only a few days, and your joy will be full.

Dear Father, You know I have been unhappy in my current situation. I've been guilty of looking at others' lives, wanting what they have, not what I have. I want to make a change right now—I need Your help in changing my attitude. Help me to have a happy, cheerful outlook in all that I do and an understanding that this is Your will for my life.

Amen.

A LIFETIME IMPACT

This is good and acceptable in the sight of God our Savior,
who desires all men to be saved and to come to
the knowledge of the truth.
—1 Tim. 2:3–4

God has given each one of us the potential to influence others for Christ. One way we do this is by living our lives for Him with godly purpose. For example, in order to raise godly children, parents must live their lives submitted to Christ. They should be men and women of faith—trusting God and praying for every need their family has. I remember when my children were young, they learned to pray for their needs. They also prayed for their family and friends, and they learned very early in life to trust God because they witnessed this as being a part of the fabric of our family's life.

My children also learned a key principle—one that I am certain helped to shape their lives in a dramatic way—and that was one of obedience. One day while I was in my study, they came in asking if they could do a certain thing. I knew from the beginning that it was not something they needed to do, but instead of telling them no—which would have saved time—I decided this was a great opportunity for them to learn how to obey God.

My son, Andy, was particularly determined and asked me to tell them what I believed God would say. I held firm and said, "I'm not going to tell you. You need to spend time with Him in prayer, and He will show you what you need to do." After a couple of hours, they reappeared at my door and wanted to know if we could talk. They had their answer, and I was eager to hear it.

"God wants us to do it," they proclaimed as both of their heads nodded in agreement. However, I knew this was not God's will. So I instructed them to go back and this time to ask Him to confirm His will in His Word. "We can't," they replied, "because we don't really think He wants us to do it, but we wanted to try anyway."

For a moment I was shocked, but almost wanted to smile at the sincerity of their confession. It was then that

I was able to tell them why I believed God was saying no. We prayed together, and as we were getting up, one of them said, "It's a lot better to obey God than to disobey and risk the outcome." It was a simple truth, but it is one that all of us need to heed.

God has a purpose for saying no. He sees the big picture of our lives and knows the very actions and events that will have devastating results if we fail to obey Him. In fact, for years I have told my children and those in my congregation these simple words: "Always obey God, and leave the consequences to Him." This means that no matter what we may face, if we are living in obedience to His plan, then we have no reason to worry.

While my mother only had a sixth-grade education, she taught me a principle that set a firm foundation in my life and that was to obey God regardless of the cost. I watched her obediently living out her faith, even when she had nothing, and her witness profoundly affected me. From my early childhood until I left home, my mother knelt by my bed each night and prayed with me.

In fact, I learned to pray, not by her instructions, but by watching her do something that came so naturally to her—praying to her Lord and Savior.

If you truly want to impact your children to live godly lives, live a godly life before them. Pray with them, and give them the opportunity to see God at work in your life. Also, take the time to influence your family by teaching them biblical truths and principles. Children will never forget the way you handled yourself in the midst of adversity, how you valued and demonstrated respect to others, or the way you gave of yourself to someone who was in need.

The events, trials, and joys that impact your life also impact theirs. When children see your generosity, they will want to imitate you. Can they fail to recall that they heard you talking about your love and concern for other people, or that they saw you weep with compassion over someone else's heartaches and difficulties? Therefore, be certain your life is pure and bright, so it will make a positive impact.

Lord, when I think back, I remember that it was the demonstration of Your love through someone else that made me yearn for You. I want to have that same impact on others. Live Your life through me, and let my conversation, conduct, and character reflect You.

Amen.

FORGIVENESS

Be kind to one another, tender-hearted, forgiving each other,
just as God in Christ also has forgiven you.
—*Eph. 4:32*

It was a memorable dinner—not for the food but for the conversation. In the dining room of our home, God was righting some wrongs between my children and me. I wanted to know if there was any unforgiveness in their hearts toward me.

My son spoke first, "Dad, do you remember the time you were in your study and I was practicing my music? I was playing the same part of a song over and over. I admit it was loud, but you came into the living room and asked, 'Is that all you know?' I felt as though you were rejecting my music and me. That hurt." Then my daughter spoke up, "When I was five years old and we lived in Miami, you sent me to my room and made me stay there for the rest of the night. I cried and cried."

They went on to share other instances when they felt I had offended them. I could have become defensive and even angry, but I didn't because I wanted them to know that there was nothing between us—just love and forgiveness. I knew there was only one thing I needed to do and that was to ask them to forgive me.

Whether you have wronged someone or a person has wronged you, forgiveness is the only way to fully experience the love of God. His love is set into motion the moment you seek the forgiveness of someone you have hurt or extend it to a person who offended you. An unforgiving spirit is poison. It stagnates Christian growth, pollutes your relationship with Jesus, and robs you of personal joy.

You can start the healing process right now by examining yourself and then repenting of any unforgiveness you have toward God or others. Thomas à Kempis writes, "We carefully count others' offenses against us, but we rarely consider what others may suffer because of us." Continue the healing process by canceling the debt of wrongs against you. This process is emotionally charged because through forgiveness we are set free to love and be loved.

Jesus actually commands us to forgive one another. Peter thought he could talk the Lord into setting a limitation on forgiveness, but he couldn't. "Peter came and said to Him, 'Lord, how often shall my brother sin against me and I forgive him? Up to seven times?' Jesus said to him, 'I do not say to you, up to seven times, but up to seventy times seven'" (Matt. 18:21–22).

God's forgiveness is limitless. And this is the same approach we are to have with others. Some who read these words have suffered deep hurt—emotionally and physically—at the hands of others. God knows the depth of these wounds. Forgiveness is not something any of us can do apart from Him. We need Him to show us how to forgive and to move past the hurt that threatens to hold us captive to feelings of depression, resentment, anger, and bitterness.

Many times, we refuse to forgive because we want our offender to suffer. God, however, tells us, "Vengeance is Mine, and retribution, in due time their foot will slip" (Deut. 32:35). When you cling to unforgiveness and anger, God cannot free you from the bondage of hurt that you are carrying.

True freedom comes when we forgive. There may be times when it is not appropriate to face those who have hurt us. However, we certainly can forgive them by the grace of God alone in prayer.

All the time you spend in the mire of unforgiveness is wasted. It counts for nothing, and it often leads to physical and emotional stress and disease. Yet the moment you forgive, the restoration process begins. Bitterness loses its hostile grip on your life, and the freedom of forgiveness is ushered in. You can never be fully free until you fully forgive.

Lord, it's incredible how past unresolved hurts can affect so much of our lives. I do not want anything to come between You and me. I know there are hurts I must deal with and correct. Please bring to my mind those past wrongs, and give me the wisdom to make them right with Your help.

Amen.

SOLVING PROBLEMS THROUGH PRAYER

*I love the LORD, because He hears my voice
and my supplications. Because He has inclined His ear to me,
therefore I shall call upon Him as long as I live.*
—Ps. 116:1–2

Two things in this world are said to be certain—death and taxes. Let me add a third—difficulty. Unlike the first two, you can do something about the trials and problems you face. You can pray. In His love, God has provided prayer as a means for us to fellowship with Him and access His wisdom for the circumstances we face.

God is in the problem-solving business, and when you present your situation to Him, He will provide a solution. His reply may or may not be what you would like to hear; it may not fit neatly into your schedule. Nonetheless, He is committed to you and has entered into a covenant relationship with you whereby He assumes the responsibility to guide, correct, and make His will known to you. Prayer is one of the ways He does this.

Present your problem to God. We don't have to be afraid of being transparent before God—He knows us completely and loves us unconditionally. He understands our problems and knows the exact steps we need to take in order to gain a solution. David poured his heart out to God and learned to trust Him in the process—we can, too. The more specific you are in prayer, the more readily you can discern His answer.

Expect God to act. God always wants us to learn how to be still, wait for His timing, and then be ready to watch Him work. He told His people to call on Him, and He would do great things (Jer. 33:3). Your petitions will seem meaningless unless you are actively looking through eyes of faith for His deliverance. This is what faith is about—watching God work mightily behind the scenes of our natural circumstances.

In his essay "The Efficacy of Prayer," C. S. Lewis writes, "If an infinitely wise Being listens to the requests of finite and foolish creatures, of course He will sometimes grant and sometimes refuse them." God's solutions are always best, even if they do not align with our desires.

Express your gratitude to the Lord. Thanksgiving acknowledges God's faithfulness and love when circumstances say otherwise. A thankful heart rejoices in the God who answers, as much as it does in the answer itself.

Never forget that God is greater than your problem and is infinitely equipped to resolve it. The power of prayer can never be overestimated because of the omnipotent God who hears and answers. Be willing to work out your difficulty His way, follow His instructions, and assume the risk that He may or may not remove the problem. In any case, your petitions will set the stage for the best possible solution when you put your trust in the God who cares.

Dear Father in heaven, thank You for the gift of prayer. That I can talk with You personally and that You listen to my petitions is nothing less than a miracle. Teach me how to communicate better with You and to trust You fully.

Amen.

TESTED AND TRUE

*[Our] momentary, light affliction is producing for us an
eternal weight of glory far beyond all comparison.*
—2 Cor. 4:17

Adversity is one of life's inescapable experiences, and it is
difficult for us to be happy when it affects us personally.
A popular theology says, "Just trust God and think
rightly; then you won't have hardship." In reading His
Word, however, we quickly learn that God uses adversity
to draw us into a closer relationship with Him. First,
trials and tribulations are not immediate signals that we
have done something wrong. Many times these come as
a natural part of life.

Second, difficulty and hardship are the very tools
God uses to teach us to trust Him to a greater degree.
He is never interested in discouraging us. Instead, He
uses trials to train us for spiritual battles that are sure to
come our way at some point.

Most of us try to avoid the subject of adversity. We just don't want to think about having to face seasons of stress or difficulty. However, it is far better to learn about adversity before you experience it than to face a hardship and wonder, *Lord, what on earth are You doing?*

We live in a fallen world, so like it or not, sin and its consequences surround us. Hardships will come, and when they do, if we fail to recall the goodness of God's love toward us, we will be tempted to become discouraged, worried, and even disillusioned. When we encounter difficulty, one of our first reactions may be to feel that what we are facing is unfair, unbelievable, and unbearable. We cry out, "It's not fair, God!" However, we should be asking, "Lord, what do You want me to learn through this difficulty?"

If we never experience persecution or trials, we will never know the depth of God's love and goodness toward us. It is in the dark times when we feel abandoned that He comes to us and gathers us up in His infinitely strong and loving arms. Without trial or tragedy, our view of God would be completely out of balance. We would never know His awesome strength poured out for us. Without adversity, we would fail to understand who He truly is or how He values us.

Do you want the kind of faith that is based only on what you can see or hear? Most of us grew up hearing these words: "Even though I walk through the valley of the shadow of death, I fear no evil, for You are with me" (Ps. 23:4). However, David's words in this psalm do not become a living reality until we find ourselves in the valley. It is then that God teaches us to know and understand that He is "my shepherd, I shall not want. He makes me lie down in green pastures; He leads me beside quiet waters. He restores my soul; He guides me in the paths of righteousness for His name's sake . . . I fear no evil, for You are with me" (Ps. 23:1–4).

Adversity has the potential to be a source of discouragement; or, if you allow God to have His perfect way, it will become His greatest tool of spiritual growth and love. How you respond to difficulty makes all the difference. Recall His goodness and remember, God has a purpose in mind for the hardship He allows to touch your life, and it always is perfectly tailored to fit His wonderful plan.

Lord, thank You for loving me and for having a plan for my life. Even though there have been times when I have questioned the suffering that has come my way, I have found myself trusting You and waiting for Your deliverance. You have encouraged me by allowing me to face difficult circumstances. While the hurt was real, You have been an unforgettable comfort to me. Though You did not author the suffering, You turned it around, giving it new meaning and purpose. Thank You for this and for never leaving me alone in my trials.

Amen.

THE POWER OF LOVE

The greatest of these is love.
—1 Cor. 13:13

Nothing rivals the power of God's love. It has the ability to heal a broken heart, repair a deep emotional wound, and mend a shattered relationship. In the end, love makes all things new. The apostle Paul understood this. He wrote, "If I speak with the tongues of men and of angels, but do not have love, I have become a noisy gong or a clanging cymbal" (1 Cor. 13:1). In other words, without the love of God in his life, he was no more than an empty tin can. The same is true for us.

On a scale of one to ten, the love of God is a ten—surpassing all other virtues in importance. Love is patient and kind—long-suffering and full of hope and encouragement. It never discourages. It always builds and refuses to tear down. It is never in a hurry. It is not forceful, demanding, or self-centered. Love waits for God's best, whenever and whatever that may be. It does not panic in the face of trial, defeat, or fear. It won't grasp for human solutions but always seeks to do God's will.

Love is kind, gentle, and understanding. It acts in the best interest of others, overlooks offenses, and is extravagant when it comes to giving to others. "It does not envy, it does not boast, it is not proud" (1 Cor. 13:4 NIV). It waits for God to promote and exalt. It credits Him for any personal success, while acknowledging the contributions of others. It always applauds the godly gain of another and does not flaunt or taunt but bends its knee in humility.

Love is not rude. It is polite and courteous—even to those who are ill-mannered, ill-tempered, and hurtful. True love is never self-seeking but thinks of others first.

Love is not irritated by the behavior of others. It refuses to judge, leaving that to God. It does not keep a mental record of offenses. Love does not delight in evil but rejoices with the truth. It meets each day with cheer and a smile. It thinks upon good things and is happy in simple obedience to God.

Paul concludes his description by writing, "Love never fails" (1 Cor. 13:8), and the love of God never will. Not only does this indicate that His love will never run out; it also means that whatever the situation, the proper response always is love. When we extend the love of God to others—especially those who have hurt and opposed us—we are set free from feelings of bitterness, anger, rejection, hostility, and unforgiveness.

Learning to love God and others the way He loves you will lead you to discover places in your heart where you would never venture on your own. One thing is for sure: when you live in the light of His love, you will come to know the intimate care of a loving heavenly Father.

Father, I want to be free! Free to love and to be loved. Please continue to teach me about the wonder of Your love for me. Show me how to accept it and then use me to demonstrate it to others. God, I love You and thank You for loving me first.

Amen.

MOTIVATED BY LOVE

Once you understand the unconditional love of God, you will find it hard to stop loving Him. You may be thinking, *Well, having done what I have done in life, or having been where I have been, how could God possibly love me?* He does because this is His nature—to love and never reject those who come to Him seeking His love and mercy.

Jesus made Himself very vulnerable by coming to earth as the Son of God. He was hurt, He felt pain, but He kept on loving. Did He stop loving Judas because of his traitor's kiss in the garden? No. He loved Judas unconditionally—betrayal or not.

Therefore, how does God want you to live? The answer

to this question is—loving Him. He also wants you to learn how to love others the way He loves. If you do this, then you can be sure that you will experience hurt along the way, you will be disappointed, and you will be rejected at times. But He faced each one of these conditions. When you have tasted genuine, unconditional love, you know it is worth the risk. It is worth the chance of being rejected. How many times? Well, it just depends on how well you have been able to receive true love.

Sadly, many people live and die never having experienced the power of genuine, unconditional love. No amount of material possessions, other relationships, exotic places to visit, prestige, prominence, prosperity, position, or power can match the awesome depth of fulfillment in experiencing God's unconditional love.

It is my prayer that over the past thirty-one days you have come to know the depth of God's love in a fresh, new way. I would urge you to pray each day with a desire to learn more about God and His wondrous love for you. Also, ask Him to give you a love for His Word that cannot be quenched. As you read it and study His principles, your life will change, and hope, joy, and peace will flood your soul. Then you will experience life at its best—daily walking in the power of His unconditional love.

GOD'S GREATEST GIFT?

Our heavenly Father has prepared many special gifts and blessings for His children, but the greatest is the gift of eternal life though His Son, Jesus. If you have never invited Him to be your Savior and Lord, you can do this right now by praying this simple prayer:

Father, I know that I am a sinner. I believe Jesus died on the cross for my sins and paid my sin debt in full. Forgive me for my sins, and cleanse me of my past failures and guilt. I surrender control of my life to You today. Make me the person You have designed me to be. I pray this in Jesus' name.

Amen.

If you sincerely prayed this to God, then according to God's Word, you have been born again! I want to challenge you to take positive steps to grow in your new faith. Tell someone of your decision to follow Jesus and find a Bible-believing church that will teach the uncompromised truth of God's Word.

Today is the first day on a journey that will someday lead you into the presence of your heavenly Father—who has loved you from the beginning of time.

OTHER BOOKS BY DR. CHARLES STANLEY

THE LIFE PRINCIPLES STUDY SERIES